Smithsonian

Amazing Animals

Silver Dolphin Books
An imprint of Printers Row Publishing Group
A division of Readerlink Distribution Services, LLC
10350 Barnes Canyon Road, Suite 100, San Diego, CA 92121
www.silverdolphinbooks.com

All notations of errors or omissions should be addressed to Silver Dolphin Books,
Editorial Department, at the above address.

ISBN: 978-1-68412-225-7

Manufactured, printed, and assembled in Stevens Point, Wisconsin, U.S.A.
Fourth printing, April 2019. WOR/04/19

23 22 21 20 19   4 5 6 7 8

Baby Animals written by Courtney Acampora
Nighttime Animals written by Brenda Scott Royce
Sea Life and *Rain Forest Animals* written by Emily Rose Oachs

Reviewed by Dr. Don E. Wilson, Curator Emeritus of the Department of Vertebrate Zoology,
National Museum of Natural History, Smithsonian.

For Smithsonian Enterprises:
Kealy Gordon, Product Development Manager, Licensing
Ellen Nanney, Licensing Manager
Brigid Ferraro, Vice President, Education and Consumer Products
Carol LeBlanc, Senior Vice President, Education and Consumer Products

Images copyright Thinkstock and SuperStock, Inc., Larisa Bishop-Boros, Mark Pellegrini.

Every effort has been made to contact copyright holders for the images in this book. If you are
the copyright holder of any uncredited image herein, please contact us at Silver Dolphin Books,
Editorial Department, 10350 Barnes Canyon Road, Suite 100, San Diego, CA 92121.

CONTENTS

A NOTE TO PARENTS AND TEACHERS

Smithsonian Readers were created for children who are just starting on the amazing road to reading. These engaging books support the acquisition of reading skills, encourage children to learn about the world around them, and help to foster a lifelong love of books. These high-interest informational texts contain fascinating, real-world content designed to appeal to beginning readers. This early access to high-quality books provides an essential reading foundation that students will rely on throughout their school career.

The five levels in the Smithsonian Readers series target different stages of learning abilities. Each child is unique; age or grade level does not determine a particular reading level.

When sharing a book with beginning readers, read in short stretches, pausing often to talk about the pictures. Have younger children turn the pages and point to the pictures and familiar words. And be sure to reread favorite parts. As children become more independent readers, encourage them to share the ideas they are reading about and to discuss ideas and questions they have. Learning practice can be further extended with the quizzes after each title.

There is no right or wrong way to share books with children. You are setting a pattern of enjoying and exploring books that will set a literacy foundation for their entire school career. Find time to read with your child, and pass on the amazing world of literacy.

Adria F. Klein, Ph.D.
Professor Emeritus
California State University, San Bernardino

SEA
LIFE

Emily Rose Oachs

CONTENTS

The Earth's Oceans

The Earth's oceans are vast and deep.

They cover two-thirds of the planet.

Earth's salty waters are divided into five different oceans.

Arctic

Pacific

Indian

Atlantic

Southern (or Antarctic)

The oceans are very important to life on Earth.

Many different kinds of animals call the ocean home.

Marine Mollusks

Mollusks are soft-bodied creatures.

Some mollusks grow hard outer shells.

Other mollusks have no shell at all.

Oysters, sea slugs, snails, squids, and octopuses are all mollusks!

Snails move using a big, flat muscle called a "foot."

The foot slowly drags them from place to place.

Giant clams are Earth's biggest mollusks.

Their shells may be more than four feet across.

They can weigh more than five hundred pounds!

Octopuses have round, soft bodies.

They can fit into tight spaces.

A fifty-pound octopus can squeeze through a two-inch hole!

Spiny Sea Urchins and Sea Stars

Sea urchins and sea stars live on the ocean floor.

They don't have eyes or brains.

Water flows through their bodies instead of blood.

Sea urchins look like spiny balls.

Sea urchins use their spines to walk and eat.

Sometimes the spines are poisonous!

Sea stars are bright colors, such as orange, blue, or purple.

They may have as many as twenty-four arms!

Sometimes a sea star loses an arm to protect itself.

A new arm will grow back in its place.

Each arm has tiny tube feet.

These tube feet help sea stars crawl and stick to surfaces.

Stinging Jellyfish

Jellyfish have bell-shaped, see-through bodies
They have long, stinging **tentacles**.
Tentacles are flexible, arm-like body parts.

Jellyfish are mostly made up of water.

They do not have brains, hearts, bones, or blood.

Most jellyfish can't swim, so they float through the ocean.

The lion's mane jellyfish is the longest animal in the world.

Its tentacles can grow to over one hundred feet!

Jellyfish use their tentacles to catch and kill food.

Box jellyfish have cube-shaped bells, or bodies.

Long tentacles grow from each of the bell's corners.

A box jellyfish's sting could kill a person.

Colorful Coral and Coral Reefs

Coral can be all different shapes, sizes, and colors.

Some corals are hard and rigid, and others are soft and flexible.

They can look like brains, feathers, or even broccoli!

Corals have tube-shaped bodies.

One end of the body attaches to a hard surface.

The other end has a mouth and stinging tentacles.

Corals live in groups, or **colonies**.

Corals die and leave their hard skeletons behind.

Over time, these skeletons build up into a coral reef.

It takes thousands of years for a coral reef to form!

Coral reefs are an important home for sea animals.

Sea horses, sharks, and other fish swim through coral reefs.

Sea Turtles: Long Distance Swimmers

Sea turtles have a hard shell and paddle-like flippers.

Sea turtles use their front flippers to swim through the ocean.

They use their back flippers to steer.

Sea turtles spend most of their lives in the water.

Many swim thousands of miles each year.

However, sea turtles swim to shore to lay their eggs.

Leatherback sea turtles don't have a hard shell.

Leatherback sea turtles have flexible, leathery shells.

They eat jellyfish, sea urchins, and squid.

Green sea turtles can swim underwater for a long time.

They can hold their breath for five hours!

Sea Anemones and Clown Fish: Ocean Friends

Sea anemones are colorful creatures.

They have soft bodies and stinging tentacles.

They attach themselves to rocks or coral reefs.

Clown fish are bright orange with white stripes.

Clown fish and sea anemones live together in the coral reef.

Sea anemones protect clown fish.

Their stinging tentacles keep clown fish **predators** away.

But clown fish are safe from a sea anemone's sting.

A special mucus covers the bodies of clown fish.

Clown fish help to keep their sea anemones clean.

They snack on sea anemones' leftovers.

Incredible Fish

Fish are animals that live in water.

Their bodies are covered in scales.

Fish use fins to swim through the water.

They use **gills** to breathe.

Fish come in many shapes, sizes, and colors.

Sharks, puffer fish, and leafy sea dragons are all fish!

Sea horses are tiny fish with tiny fins.

They curl their tails around sea grasses.

This keeps them from floating away!

Sailfish have long, sword-like noses.

They are the ocean's fastest fish.

They leap out of the ocean at almost seventy miles per hour!

Sharks: Fierce Fish

Many sharks are fierce fish.

Hundreds of sharp teeth may line their mouths.

Sharks live throughout the ocean, from its depths to shallow coastal waters.

Sharks' skeletons are made of **cartilage** instead of bones.

Cartilage is a strong, flexible tissue.

A human's nose and ears are made of cartilage.

Great white sharks' mouths have three hundred razor-sharp teeth.

Their powerful bite quickly kills their large **prey**.

Tiger sharks are violent, fierce ocean predators.

Their curved teeth rip through the shells of sea turtles.

Nurse sharks swim slowly through the coral reefs.

They eat fish, shrimp, and crabs from the ocean floor.

Rays: Flat Fish

Rays have flat, circular bodies.

Their fins spread like wings from their bodies.

Some rays have a sharp spine on their tail.

Manta rays move by flapping their fins like wings.

Sometimes they leap out of the water!

Stingrays often rest on the ocean floor.

Sand partly covers their bodies.

This hides them from predators.

Electric rays have special organs.

These organs produce electrical shocks!

Electric rays use the shocks for **defense** and catching prey.

Life in the Deep Sea

In some places, the ocean floor is miles beneath the water's surface.

These are the deepest parts of the ocean.

There the world is cold and dark.
But many sea creatures still live there.

Fangtooth fish have sharp teeth and poor eyesight.

They swim around until they bump into prey.

Animals in the deep sea rarely see daylight.

Some deep sea animals create their own light.

Anglerfish have a long spine on their head.
The tip of the spine lights up.
The spine is like a fishing pole.
Its light attracts prey to the anglerfish.

Dolphins and Porpoises: Breathing with Blowholes

Dolphins and porpoises are mammals that live in the ocean.

Mammals can't breathe underwater.

They must swim to the ocean's surface to breathe.

Dolphins and porpoises breathe using **blowholes**.

Blowholes are nostrils on top of their head.

Porpoises are speedy swimmers.

They have thicker bodies than dolphins.

Porpoises also have blunter noses and smaller mouths than dolphins do.

Dolphins make noises to talk to other dolphins.

They whistle, click, chirp, and slap their tails.

These mean they are happy, sad, scared, or want to play.

Whales: The Ocean's Largest

Like dolphins and porpoises, whales are mammals that live in the ocean.

Whales' bodies have a thick layer of fat, called **blubber**.

Blubber keeps them warm in cold waters.

Whales are some of the largest animals in the ocean.

Blue whales are the biggest animals on Earth.

Their tongues are as heavy as an elephant!

Orcas are fierce hunters.

Their four-inch-long teeth slice through their prey.

Orcas hunt and travel in groups called **pods**.

Humpback whales make low, song-like noises in the ocean.

These whales may sing for hours.

They use the songs to talk to other humpback whales.

Flying, Floating, and Diving: Sea Birds

Some birds also make their home by the sea.

They fly above it, float on it, and dive in it.

These birds rely on the ocean for survival.

Pelicans use a pouch under their bill to catch fish.

They scoop up fish in the pouch.

Then they drain the water and swallow the fish whole.

Oystercatchers wade along the ocean coasts.

They use their strong, flat bill to open mollusk shells.

Penguins huddle together on the ice in the Antarctic Ocean.

Penguins can't fly, but they are excellent swimmers.

Sometimes penguins slide across the ice on their bellies!

SEA LIFE QUIZ

1. The Earth's oceans cover how much of the planet?

   a) One-fourth

   b) Two-thirds

   c) One-half

2. How long does it take for a coral reef to form?

   a) Thousands of years

   b) One week

   c) One day

3. Which ocean creature helps protect clown fish?

   a) Sea star

   b) Sea urchin

   c) Sea anemone

4. What do fish use to breathe?

a) Nose

b) Tail

c) Gills

5. Which animal is a mammal?

a) Dolphin

b) Shark

c) Jellyfish

6. Which animals use songs to talk to each other?

a) Penguins

b) Humpback whales

c) Great white sharks

GLOSSARY

Blowholes: holes on the top of the heads of some ocean mammals used for breathing

Blubber: a layer of fat

Cartilage: a tough, flexible material

Colonies: groups of coral growing together

Defense: protecting against attack

Gills: organs on fish that let them get oxygen from the water to breathe

Pods: groups of whales

 **Predators:** animals that kill and eat other animals

Prey: an animal that is hunted or killed by another animal for food

Tentacles: flexible, arm-like body parts that are used for grabbing and moving

NIGHTTIME ANIMALS

Brenda Scott Royce

CONTENTS

Creatures of the Night

When the sun sets at night, many animals are just beginning their day.

Nighttime animals wait until dark to eat, hunt, travel, or play.

Animals that are active at night are called **nocturnal** animals.

Nocturnal animals come in all shapes, sizes, and types.

They have special features that help them get around in the dark.

Keeping Cool

Many animals are active at night because it is too hot during the day.

Wombats live in some of the hottest parts of Australia.

They spend their days in underground holes or tunnels called **burrows**.

The sidewinder glides sideways across the desert sand. In the hot months, these snakes only come out at night, when the sand is cool.

Kangaroo rats live in the desert.

They hide underground during the day, and come out at night when it is cooler.

Kangaroo rats use pouches on their cheeks to carry seeds back to their burrows.

These little rats hop upright on their back legs.

They use their long tails for balance, just like kangaroos!

Lying Low

Some animals are safer at night.

They come out after dark when there are fewer **predators** around.

A predator is an animal that eats another animal for food.

In the daytime, hedgehogs hide in holes or under piles of leaves.

At nighttime, they eat insects and small animals.

Short, sharp spines on the hedgehog's body are extra protection.

The opossum stays out of sight during the day. At night it searches for food.

Opossums sometimes look for food in backyards, gardens, and garbage cans.

When an opossum is really scared, it will play dead!

Nighttime Hunters

For a tiger, nighttime is the best time to hunt.

A tiger's stripes help it blend in with the shadows of the dark forest.

A tiger may travel several miles in a single night tracking its **prey**.

Prey is an animal that is eaten by another animal for food.

predator and prey

Alligators can remain still for hours, waiting for prey to come near.

An alligator drifting in the water looks like a log.

This helps it sneak up on its prey.

Rattlesnakes are excellent night hunters.
But they cannot see well in the dark.
Rattlesnakes have heat-sensing pits on each side of their heads.
These pits sense the body heat of rodents and other animals.

moth

The whippoorwill loves to eat moths.

Moths come out at night, so that is when the whippoorwill goes hunting.

This small bird flies with its mouth wide open to catch moths and other bugs.

Midnight Snackers

The hippopotamus is big and powerful.
It doesn't have to hide from predators.

During the day, a hippo sleeps in the water.

At night, it comes ashore to eat grass and plants.

Some creatures come out at night when there is less **competition** for food.

The black-crowned night heron fishes at night, when larger herons are asleep.

moth

Moths and butterflies are a lot alike.

Moths and butterflies are both winged insects that drink nectar from flowers.

Butterflies are daytime creatures.

Moths come out at night.

This way, there are enough flowers to go around.

Big Eyes

Special eyes help night creatures see in the dark.

The tarsier is a tiny animal with enormous eyes.

Each of the tarsier's eyes is larger than its brain!

The tarsier's big eyes help it see in the dark.

Tarsiers spend most of their time in the trees, like their monkey relatives.

At night, they search for their favorite food—insects.

Ocelots have a special layer in their eyes that helps them see in the dark.

Ocelots hunt for mice, rats, and other small animals at night.

These wild cats are great climbers and strong swimmers.

Tree frogs need good vision so they can leap from branch to branch in the dark.

Awesome Ears

Large ears help nighttime animals hear well. The bat-eared fox points its enormous ears toward the ground to listen for sounds made by insects. When it hears insects below the ground, the fox starts digging.

Termites are the bat-eared fox's favorite food.

One bat-eared fox can eat more than a million termites in a single year!

termites

Jackrabbits have very good hearing.

Their big ears help jackrabbits hear approaching predators.

Tap, tap, tap. The aye-aye taps on a tree branch...then listens carefully.

The aye-aye uses his big ears to tell if the branch has a hole.

The aye-aye knows that insects hide in tree holes.

The aye-aye uses its long finger to pry a bug out of its hiding place.

Super Noses

A good sense of smell helps nighttime animals find food, stay away from danger, and find friends in the dark.

The two-toed sloth has a very good sense of smell.

This slow-moving animal lives high up in the trees and mainly eats leaves.

Most night birds have good eyesight, but the kiwi does not.

The kiwi uses its excellent sense of smell to find food.

The kiwi uses nostrils on the tip of its beak to find worms underground.

The Baird's tapir uses its long nose to search for food at night.

Moths don't have noses but they do have a good sense of smell.

Their antennae work like noses to detect smells.

Some flowers bloom only at night, when bees and butterflies are resting.

These flowers need moths and bats to spread their **pollen**.

The sweet smell of evening primrose attracts moths.

53

Whiskers and Webs

The sense of touch is very important to nighttime animals.

Many nighttime animals have long, thick whiskers on their faces.

Whiskers help nighttime animals find their way in the dark.

The leopard's long, thick whiskers are very sensitive.

Whiskers help the leopard find food and keep the leopard from bumping into things in the dark!

Black widow spiders build webs of strong silk.

At night, the female black widow sits in the center of her web.

She waits for an insect to get tangled in the silky strands.

When an insect enters the web, the silk threads shake.

The shaking tells the black widow that she has trapped her next meal.

Night Flight

β

Many types of birds migrate, or travel long distances, at certain times of the year.

Most migrating birds fly at night.

At night, the air is cooler and calmer, and there are fewer predators.

How do birds find their way in the dark?

They use the moon and stars to guide them!

The patterns formed by stars are like maps in the sky for migrating birds.

Songbirds make many sounds while migrating.

Their songs help them stick together in the dark and warn other birds about danger.

Fireflies light up the night sky.

Fireflies' bellies have a built-in light source.

Fireflies flash their lights to locate each other in the dark.

Bats

Bats may have the best hearing of all the animals.

The large pointed ears of the Virginia big-eared bat look like funnels and help gather sound.

Bats can hear high-pitched noises that people cannot hear.

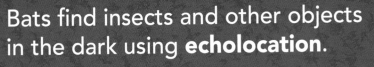

Bats find insects and other objects in the dark using **echolocation**.

They send out high-pitched sounds.

The sounds bounce off nearby objects.

The bat can identify the object and where it is by the sound of its echo.

Owls

Owls hunt for mice and other small animals at night.

Owls' curved wings and soft feathers let them fly without making a sound.

Swooping down silently, they catch prey by surprise.

Owls' super-sized eyes are made for night hunting.

Owls can't move their eyes in their sockets as people do.

Instead they rotate their heads to see around them.

Like many
night owls,
the barn owl has
mismatched ears!

One ear is bigger, and one is smaller.

One ear is higher on the owl's head
than the other.

This helps the owl quickly pinpoint the
source of sounds.

Then barn owls can catch their prey in
total darkness.

Night Noises

noisy tokay gecko

Nighttime animals can be very noisy.

Owls hoot, coyotes howl, frogs croak, and crickets chirp.

In the dark, animals make sounds to find friends or frighten enemies.

croaking bullfrog

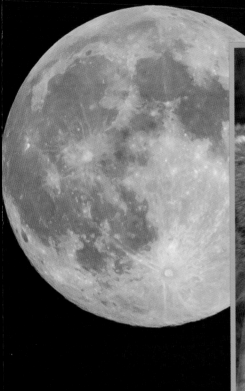

Coyote families
are called packs.

At night, the packs
hunt together.

Coyote packs
howl to say: "This
is our space."

Daytime Sleepers

When the sun rises, nighttime animals look for a safe place to sleep.

Some find shelter underground. Others prefer the trees.

Some hide under bushes or in tall grass.

Sugar gliders nest in trees.

Up to twelve sugar gliders may share one nest.

A two-toed sloth sleeps between the branches of a tree.

Its brown hair helps it blend in.

Some nighttime animals don't need to hide during the day.

Alligators like to bask in the sun at the water's edge.

Leopards have excellent balance.

These large cats can sleep on tree branches without falling off.

By the time the sun is high up in the sky, most nighttime animals are fast asleep.

When darkness falls, they'll come out again...to eat, hunt, travel, and play.

NIGHTTIME ANIMALS QUIZ

1. What are animals that are active at night called?

a) Mammals

b) Nocturnal

c) Special

2. Where do hippopotamuses sleep during the day?

a) In a tree

b) In the grass

c) In the water

3. Which animal has eyes larger than its brain?

a) Tarsier

b) Bat-eared fox

c) Kiwi

4. What is a bat-eared fox's favorite food?

a) Fruit

b) Grass

c) Termites

5. Which insect lights up the night sky?

a) Firefly

b) Termite

c) Black widow spider

6. How do bats find insects and other objects in the dark?

a) Scent

b) Touch

c) Echolocation

GLOSSARY

Burrows: holes or tunnels dug in the ground by an animal for shelter

Competition: the act of two or more kinds of animals looking for the same resource such as food or territory

Echolocation: a method bats use to find objects using sound waves

Nocturnal: active at night

Pollen: powder on a flower that when moved to a different flower, helps make a new flower

Predators: animals that hunt other animals for food

Prey: an animal that is hunted by other animals for food

* Smithsonian

Rain Forest Animals

Emily Rose Oachs

Contents

What Is a Rain Forest?

The rain forest is warm
and wet.
More rain falls here than
anywhere else on Earth.

Hundreds of species of plants, animals,
and insects live among the trees.
Only six percent of the Earth is
rain forest. But almost half of
Earth's plants and animals
call it home!

DID YOU KNOW?

Central and South
America, Africa,
Southeast Asia,
and Australia all
have rain forests.

Giants of the Rain Forest

Some of the rain forest's smallest animals live in the treetops. The larger animals live on the forest floor.

black leopard

The cassowary is the rain forest's largest bird. It is over five feet tall! Cassowaries kick at **predators** with their powerful legs.

The green anaconda is the heaviest snake on Earth. It weighs over five hundred pounds and grows to over thirty feet long. The green anaconda is a fast swimmer!

African forest elephants are the rain forest's biggest animals. They eat leaves, bark, and fruit.

? DID YOU KNOW?

Some fruits only forest elephants can open. The elephants stab the tough shells with their tusks.

Incredible Insects

spiny bush cricket

The rain forest teems with tiny critters: insects! There are an estimated thirty million different species of tropical bugs.

Insects are important to the rain forest's growth. Many insects eat dead and dying plants. This breaks down plants and brings **nutrients** to the soil.

glasswing butterfly

Leaf-cutter ants march through the rain forest carrying pieces of leaves. They bring the leaves to their nests to grow fungus.

? DID YOU KNOW?

Nearly one thousand species of beetles have been counted on a single rain forest tree!

Dung beetles pack monkey dung into balls. Then the beetles bury the dung. Some dung beetles feast on this ball of manure!

Lizards: Rain Forest Reptiles

Lizards are a type of **reptile**. Reptiles are "cold-blooded" animals with scaly skin.

Green basilisk lizards go on tree branches hanging over water. If disturbed, green basilisk lizards don't swim to safety. Instead, they sprint across the water's surface!

If threatened, green iguanas lash out at predators with their sharp tails. If a predator catches their tail, the iguana can leave it and grow a new one.

Draco lizards leap out of the trees and glide through the air. They leap to find food or safety. In the air, Draco lizards spread their ribs like wings.

Forest Frogs

Not all frogs live near water in the rain forest. Frogs need to stay moist to breathe through their skin. The rain forest's wet air keeps these **amphibians** from drying out.

Some rain forest frogs live in trees. They cling to tree trunks with the sticky pads on their toes.

Mantellas are brightly colored, poisonous frogs.

The tiny glass frog is only a little over an inch long. It has a see-through belly.

Red-eyed tree frogs are colorful **amphibians**. They have orange feet, green skin, blue legs, and red eyes.

Sly Snakes

Snakes slither on the rain forest floor looking for food.

Snakes kill their **prey** in different ways. Boas, anacondas, and pythons are constrictors. Constrictors squeeze their prey.

Vipers and cobras kill with **venomous** bites. Their fangs release poison into their prey.

Emerald tree boas are **nocturnal** constrictors. Their bodies look like vines in the rain forest!

Paradise tree snakes glide through the air. To glide, they launch themselves from tree branches. Then they spread their ribs to flatten their body.

DID YOU KNOW?

A paradise tree snake can glide more than three hundred feet through the rain forest!

Canopy Camouflage

Camouflage is an animal's coloring that helps it blend in with the background. Camouflage keeps animals hidden. Camouflage helps animals hunt for a meal.

Can you see the jaguar?

Colorful birds hide among flowers.

This leaf is actually an insect!

In the rain forest, light passes through the **canopy**. Ocelots have golden fur and black spots. Their coloring looks like the spotted sunlight on the forest floor.

Walking sticks look like twigs. They look like sticks moving in the breeze!

Parson's chameleons are usually yellow, teal, and green. They can change their coloring to blend into their surroundings. Parson's chameleons also change their coloring because of the temperature or their mood.

Mammals in the Treetops

lemurs

Many mammals live in the canopy. Mammals are animals with hairy bodies. They have backbones and give birth to live babies. Humans are also mammals.

Binturongs are furry, shaggy mammals. They are so big that they have to climb down to the forest floor to move to a new tree.

Sloths are slow-moving mammals. They sleep up to eighteen hours a day! Some sloths hang upside down.

Aye-ayes have a long, clawed middle finger. They tap this finger against trees to find food.

Monkeys: Playful Primates

Many monkeys spend all their time in trees. Monkeys swing from branch to branch.

? DID YOU KNOW?

Monkeys' feet have thumbs—just like their hands! With these thumbs, monkeys can grasp with both their hands and feet.

Monkeys have long, furry tails. They help monkeys balance on tree branches.

Pygmy marmosets grow to just five inches. They are the world's smallest monkeys.

Mandrills have stubby tails and live on the forest floor. Mandrills have red and blue faces and brightly colored behinds!

Capuchin monkeys leap from tree to tree. Sometimes they hang from trees by their tails!

Monkeys are smart and curious. They often live in large troops with other monkeys. They communicate using barks, grunts, and wails.

? DID YOU KNOW?

Monkeys are **primates**—like you! Primates are known for their intelligence, large brains, and opposable thumbs.

Proboscis monkeys are famous for their long, dangling noses. But they are also excellent swimmers.

Howler monkeys are louder than any other monkey. Their voices echo through the rain forest for miles!

Spider monkeys have long limbs and tails. They swing arm over arm through the trees.

Amazing Apes

Apes are hairy-bodied primates. They live in the forests of Africa and Southeast Asia.

Apes are very smart creatures. They sometimes use simple tools! Chimpanzees use stones like a hammer to crack open fruits and nuts.

Apes and monkeys can be hard to tell apart. Apes have larger brains and bodies. Apes don't have tails.

Monkeys have tails.   Apes do not have tails.

Apes have long arms. Gorillas, chimpanzees, and bonobos walk on their knuckles.

Orangutans' arms almost reach their ankles when they stand. Their arms can be seven feet across!

Butterflies: Fluttering through the Rain Forest

Lots of species of butterflies flutter through the rain forest. Their wings can be very colorful.

Butterflies use their long mouths to sip the nectar from flowers. Sometimes butterflies fly to the forest floor. They drink juices from fallen fruit.

A blue morpho's underside is brown. The tops of its wings are an electric blue.

The Queen Alexandra's birdwing is the biggest butterfly on Earth. It has a twelve-inch wingspan!

A monarch butterfly's orange color is a warning. It lets predators know that they're poisonous.

Birds: Color in the Canopy

The canopy forms a high roof over the rain forest. Colorful and noisy birds perch in the canopy.

Birds fly to branches with ripe, juicy fruit. Insects fly in the canopy. Insects are also a favorite meal for birds.

Toucans are known for their huge, brightly colored bills. Their bills can grow to one-third of the bird's length. To sleep, toucans tuck their bill down their back.

Macaws, Amazons, parakeets, and cockatoos are all types of parrots. Up to one thousand of these bright birds may form into a flock!

Up in the Air: Forest Fliers

High in the treetops, animals swoop, dive, and soar through the leaves.

Hummingbirds hover near flowers to drink nectar. They can beat their wings up to seventy times per second!

A harpy eagle's wingspan spreads six feet from tip to tip! They grab prey with their sharp, strong **talons**.

At night, another forest flier comes out—bats!

Vampire bats pierce the flesh of their prey with razor-sharp teeth. Then they drink blood from the wound. Their teeth are so sharp that their prey sometimes don't realize they've been bitten!

Rain Forest Animals Quiz

1. What is the largest bird in the rain forest?

   (a) Macaw
   (b) Ostrich
   (c) Cassowary

2. Lizards are what type of animal?

   (a) Reptile
   (b) Mammal
   (c) Amphibian

3. Which animal uses its long middle finger to find insects in trees?

   (a) Sloth
   (b) Draco Lizard
   (c) Aye-aye

4. Which snake is NOT a constrictor?

   (a) Cobra
   (b) Boa
   (c) Anaconda

5. Which is NOT a mammal?

   (a) Monkey
   (b) Mantella
   (c) Sloth

6. Which animal can change its coloring to match its surroundings?

   (a) Parson's chameleon
   (b) Draco lizard
   (c) Ocelot

Answers: 1. c 2. a 3. c 4. a 5. b 6. a

Glossary

amphibians animals that can live in water and on land

canopy top of forest that forms a kind of roof

nocturnal active at night

predators animals that hunt other animals for food

prey animal that is hunted by other animals for food

primates types of mammals that have hands that can grasp, forward-facing eyes, and often live in trees

reptile cold-blooded animal such as a snake or lizard

talons bird's claws

venomous filled with poison

BABY ANIMALS

Courtney Acampora

CONTENTS

Baby Animals

Baby animals come in all shapes and sizes.

Some are small and some are big.

Baby animals can have feathers, soft fur, or no hair at all!

Some babies stay with their mothers their whole lives.

Baby animals follow their mothers to learn about the world.

Lions

Cozy Koalas

Koalas are not bears.

Koalas are **marsupials**.

Marsupials are animals that have pouches.

Marsupial mothers carry the young in their pouches.

Baby koalas are called joeys.

Joeys are the size of a jellybean when they are born!

Joeys crawl into their mother's pouch to grow.

Joeys drink their mother's milk in the pouch.

Joeys leave the pouch when they are seven months old.

Then they ride on their mother's back.

At one year old, joeys can climb trees and eat leaves.

Big Baby Elephants

A baby elephant is called a calf.

Elephant calves are some of the biggest babies on Earth!

When they are born, they are three feet tall and weigh two hundred pounds!

Baby elephants are part of a **her**

A herd is a group of female elephants and their calves.

A herd protects the babies.

Baby elephants drink their mother's milk.

When they are two or three years old, they eat grass.

They use their trunks to grab the grass.

Male calves stay with their mothers until they are teenagers.

Female calves stay with their mothers their whole lives.

Part of the Troop: Gorilla Babies

A baby gorilla only weighs four pounds at birth.

The baby's mother carries it against her chest.

When it is older, the baby rides on its mother's back through the forest.

Gorillas are **mammals**.

Mammals are warm-blooded, produce milk, and give birth to live young.

Baby gorillas learn to walk when they are five months old.

Baby gorillas like to climb on trees!

Their mother builds a nest of leaves to sleep in every night.

Baby gorillas share a nest with their mother.

A Lion's Pride and Joy

A baby lion is called a cub.
Cubs live in a **pride**.
A pride is a group of lions.

Mother lions give birth to three or four babies at a time.

Cubs sleep and play with their mother and other cubs.

Cubs start hunting at eleven months old.

Male cubs start growing a mane at one year old.

A mane is the long hair that grows around their head.

Pandas: Bamboo Babies

Baby pandas are very small when they are born.

They are pink, hairless, and blind.

Panda cubs depend on their mothers.

Baby pandas are helpless for their first three months.

The mother panda holds the baby in her paw.

She holds the baby panda close.

Baby pandas grow and play with their mother.

Baby pandas eat bamboo when they are seven months old.

Bamboo is their favorite food.

Tiny Turtles

Baby turtles are **reptiles**.

Reptiles are cold-blooded, don't have hair, and lay eggs.

Snakes, lizards, and crocodiles are reptiles too.

snake   lizard   crocodile

A mother turtle digs a nest on a beach.

She lays her eggs and covers the nest with sand.

Then she goes back to the ocean.

114

In about sixty days, baby turtles break through their shells.

They crawl out of their nest and head to the ocean.

In the ocean, they find food and grow strong.

Cuddly Bear Cubs

Baby brown bears are called cubs.

Cubs are born in January and February.

Cubs are born in a **den**.

A den is a place for animals to rest during winter.

Two cubs are born at one time.

Cubs are born without hair and teeth.

They snuggle against their mother's fur to keep warm.

Cubs follow their mother out of the den in the spring.

Darling Dolphins

A baby dolphin is called a calf.
A mother dolphin has one calf at a time.
Sometimes, a mother dolphin has twins.

A dolphin is a mammal.
An ocean mammal must come up
to the surface to breathe.
The mother dolphin takes the calf
to the surface for its first breath.

The calf drinks its mother's milk for up to two years.

It learns to swim by staying close to its mother.

It learns to play by chasing other dolphins and tossing seaweed.

A calf stays with its mother for up to eight years.

Nesting Owl Chicks

An owl is a bird.

Birds have feathers, lay eggs, and most can fly.

A baby owl is called a chick.

The mother owl lays eggs in a nest.

The mother sits on the eggs to keep them warm.

The chicks hatch from their eggs!
Their mother protects and feeds
the chicks in the nest.

Owls are **nocturnal**.

Nocturnal means awake and active
at night.

Chicks learn to hunt and fly at night.

Giraffes Standing Tall

A baby giraffe is called a calf.

A baby giraffe learns to walk when it's only one hour old!

A calf drinks its mother's milk.

When a calf is four months old it eats leaves.

The calf joins other babies.

They learn to play together.

One of the mothers watches the calves so they are protected from **predators**.

A predator is an animal that kills and eats other animals for food.

Predators

Playful Pups: Sea Otters

Sea otters are playful animals.

They like to wrestle and chase their tail.

Baby sea otters are called pups.

Sea otter pups have special hair that helps them float in the water.

At first, a pup cannot swim.

The pup floats on its mother's belly.

The mother otter dives down to get food for the pup.

The pup floats at the surface wrapped in kelp.

After two months, the pup learns to swim on its own.

Spotted Babies: Cheetahs

Baby cheetahs are called cubs.

A mother cheetah usually gives birth to three to five cubs at one time.

Cubs are born w
spots on their fu

The spots **camouflage** the cubs in the grass

Camouflage help animals hide and blend in.

Their mother moves the cubs every few days.

The cubs are moved so they are protected from predators.

The cubs live with their mother for two years.

Their mother teaches them how to hunt and play.

Hold on Tight, Baby Chimpanzee!

Chimpanzees are a type of ape.

An ape is a mammal similar to a monkey, but without a tail.

Chimpanzees are closely related to humans.

Baby chimpanzees are born with pink skin and dark hair.

Baby chimpanzees have a white tail tuft.

When they get older, the tail tuft disappears.

Baby chimpanzees hold onto their mothers' bellies.

They also ride on their mothers' backs like a piggyback ride!

Baby chimpanzees drink their mother's milk until they are three years old.

They live with their mothers for up to ten years.

BABY ANIMALS QUIZ

1. What are marsupials?
a) Animals with no hair
b) Animals that eat other animals
c) Animals that have pouches

2. What is a pride?
a) An animal that eats plants
b) A group of lions
c) A mammal

3. What is a panda's favorite food?
a) Grass
b) Bamboo
c) Meat

4. Which animal is nocturnal?
a) Owl
b) Dolphin
c) Giraffe

5. What helps animals hide?
a) Nocturnal
b) Predators
c) Camouflage

6. Which animal is closely related to humans?
a) Cheetah
b) Chimpanzee
c) Gorilla

Answers: 1) c 2) b 3) b 4) a 5) c 6) b

GLOSSARY

Camouflage: an animal's coloring that helps it hide and blend in

Den: a place for animals to rest in the winter

Herd: a group of animals, such as elephants

Mammals: animals that are warm-blooded, covered in hair, and give birth to live young

Marsupials: mammals with a pouch to carry their young

Nocturnal: awake and active at night

Predators: animals that survive by killing and eating other animals

Pride: a group of lions

Reptiles: animals that are cold-blooded, lay eggs, and are covered in scales